Four Sneaky Kittens

Violet Crabtree Mackie

Willow, my cat, is the Boss of our house.

It's been a long time since we've seen a mouse.

She isn't afraid in the night, or the day.

Not just inside but outdoors at play.

A big feral cat came to our yard one night.

There was growling and yowling … then it was quiet.

Willow comes with us when we go for a stroll.

Maybe she thinks she's A Cat On Patrol.

You might not believe that but it's honestly true

along with the fact that her fur is a quite blue.

Wouldn't you know last time we roamed about,

Willow started having kittens while we were out!

Those sneaky kittens wanted to arrive in a hurry

I grabbed Willow and took off home in a scurry.

Then, there wasn't just one… there were more!

Not two, or even three—there were four!

Their meowing is squeaky, their eyes shut tight.

They seem to be hungry all day and all night.

And one sneaky kitten starts to creep,

up onto her mother while the others sleep.

Were they girls or boys? We didn't know.

I didn't want to wait for them to grow.

The lady next door is an expert on cats.

She came right over and helped us sort that.

Their eyes are closed; their meowing is squeaky,

but those four tiny kittens like being sneaky.

Quiet as a whisper ,they wriggle away.

They can't see but they still don't stay.

With their floppy heads bobbing around.

Those four sneaky kittens are quickly found.

They stumble and fumble, bumping each other.

Then those sneaky kittens fall asleep on each another.

Their mother doesn't like them piled up that way.

She lines them up straight and hopes they will stay...

But sleep is something needed by a tired mother,

and those sneaky kittens are all over each other.

Slowly their eyes open, the world to see.

They don't miss a chance to roam free.

Those kittens sneak off with a secret wish.

To nibble tuna from their mother's dish.

I thought they'd have a tummy ache for sure,

eating grownup cat food—but they want more!

Those kittens just fall asleep on each other.

Then wake up for more milk from their mother.

With a rough pink tongue Willow licks their fur,

cleaning and preening her babies till they purr.

I cuddle those kittens when Willow doesn't mind,

She lets us pet them as long as we're kind.

Poking and snuffling, they always want to play.

It doesn't matter how near, or far away,

But I know it is soon that they will grow.

Before long they will find other places to go.

Our toys won't be safe from their little paws.

Couches won't be safe from tiny, sharp claws.

Copyright © Violet Crabtree Mackie 2018

All rights reserved. Without limiting the rights under copyright reserved above, no part of this work/publication may be reproduced, stored in or introduced into a retrieval system, or transmitted, in any form or by any means (electronic, mechanical, print, photocopying, recording or otherwise), without the prior written permission of the copyright owner.

As told to Nanna Nonna — Linda Ruth Brooks

Cover & Interior Design: *Linda Ruth Brooks Publishing*

lindaruthbrooks@bigpond.com

ISBN: 978-0-6482985-4-0

Fiction/juvenile/cats

Four Sneaky Kittens is *almost* a work of fiction. Any similarity between the characters in this book and real cats, living or dead, is not quite coincidental. This book can be purchased at online bookstores, retail outlets

www.ingramcontent.com/pod-product-compliance
Lightning Source LLC
Chambersburg PA
CBRC091203070526
44583CB00009B/191